TRANSFORMED FROM GLORY TO GLORY

REV. SAMUEL O. AKANDE

TRANSFORMED FROM GLORY TO GLORY

Written by:

REV. SAMUEL O. AKANDE
akandesamuel481@gmail.com

ISBN: 978-978-998-235-6

Published by:

COMMUNE WRITERS INT'L

www.communewriters.com

+234 8139 260 389

TABLE OF CONTENTS

DEDICATION

I dedicate this book to the Almighty God, the source of all glory. Who inspired and empowered me to write this piece.

I dedicate it to my parents; Chief Oladapo Akande and late Mrs. Oladunni Akande. For their efforts over me.

ACKNOWLEDGEMENT

I want to thank everyone who has been a blessing to me one way or the other, in the past and now.

My special thanks to my spiritual Father, Rev. Dr. Emmanuel Adebola, who encouraged me to write this book.

To a wonderful Daddy, Pastor Oloye, for his love and care.

To my wife, Pastor Mrs. Rachael, thank you for your unending love and support.

To the trustees of our ministry, most especially our secretary, thank you for your loyalty and labor of love.

To the elders and members of our ministry, most especially my covenant partners, thanks for your support and labor of love.

To Daddy and mummy Idowu Ekundayo, thank you for your care and love.

To a friend that sticks closer than a brother, Pastor Folorunso Elegbede, thanks for always being there.

To the editor of this book, and every individual who contributed towards the production of it.

Thank you.

May the LORD bless you richly in Jesus mighty name.

INTRODUCTION

Glory gives value to human life, a life without glory is a valueless one. The good part of the story is that there is no one created into this world without glory. Glory differs from each other, no glory is exactly like another. This difference is what makes each glory unique and outstanding. God created you to stand out of the crowd. To be outstanding, your glory must shine for the world to see.

A glory that fails to manifest is a great loss to humanity, because God sent each of us to this world, to manifest our glory, to make the world a better place. A man of glory is a problem solver. Anyone who wants to be someone prominent in life must be well equipped with the knowledge of how to discover, develop and manifest his or her glory for the world to see. This book will teach you how to do that. It will also reveal to you the different dimensions of God's glory, the things you must do to move from one level of glory to another.

It is my fervent prayer that as you read this book, you will be transformed into a higher level of glory in Jesus' mighty name.

Amen.

1

WHAT IS GLORY?

God is the embodiment of glory, everything about God is glorious. He is the source of all glory. From Him comes all glory and to Him all glory return.

God is covered in glory, it is this glory that announces his presence wherever He goes. When you see this glory of God, you have seen God.

Glory is the manifestation of God's presence, as perceived by humans.

Glory, derived from the Greek word Doxa and the Hebrew word *kavod* meaning; power, majesty, praise, honor, dignity, great light, excellence, wisdom, authority, holiness, and state of absolute happiness.

Living in glory is experienced when you receive the highlighted privileges from people.

1. PRAISES: When people praise you often, either as a result of a good job you did, your achievements, or your status, it is an indication that you are in glory, and your glory is shining for all to see. You are receiving constant praises because glory attracts praises. Where there are praises, there is glory and vice versa. "But thou art holy, o thou that inhabitest the praises of Isreal"

(Psalm 22:3). God who is the source of all glory dwells in praises. (Psalm 22:3) confirms it, likewise, anyone whose glory is shining is endeared with praises.

2. WORSHIP: Glory attracts worship, when you are in glory, people will worship you. To worship is to show respect, love, and devotion to someone/cause. When you are in glory, people will devote, their time and efforts to support your vision. Loyalty is a part of worship, glory makes people loyal to you. "Thy people shall be willing in the day of thy power…" (Psalm 110:3). What that scripture is saying is that, on the day of your glory, people will be willing to devote their time and efforts to serve you.

3. ADMIRATION: When people constantly admire you, it is because they see glory on you, a shining one. The glory seen in you is the object of admiration. As a result of this glory, people will see you as a wonderful person. "But the men marveled, saying, what manner of man is this, that even the winds and the sea obey him!" (Matthew 8:27). The disciples of Jesus admired him greatly because of the glory of God in his life. To admire someone is to feel respect and approval for someone, show positive emotion towards the person, and regard such a person as a wonderful being.

4. SUBMISSION: This is the act of accepting or yielding to a superior force or the will or authority of another person. Submission, in this case, is not by coercion, it is to yield yourself to the authority of another person willingly. When people see glory in your life, they will willingly submit to your authority. "Then all Israel gathered themselves to David unto Hebron, saying, behold, we are thy bone and thy flesh" (1 Chronicle 11:1). In the above scripture, the children of Israel willingly submitted themselves to the authority of David, because they saw glory in his life.

5. PROTECTION: It is the process of keeping something or someone safe. People always protect the person whose glory is shining and affecting others positively. The reason is that people do not want that glory to be truncated because it is blessing many lives. "But the people answered, Thou shalt not go forth: for if we flee away, they will not care for us; neither if half of us die, will they care for us: but thou art worth ten thousand of us: therefore now thou should succor us out of the city" (2 Samuel 18:3). When the men of David were about to go to war with the men of Absalom his son who rebelled against his father's authority, they pleaded with him not to go to war with them, because they don't want him (the glory of Israel) to die untimely. If your glory is affecting life positively, people will be ready to lay down their lives to protect you.

6. CARE: It is the state of being cared for by others. If people see glory in you, they will make provision for your welfare. So that you can have time to be of more benefit to them. "And Joanna the wife of Chuza Herod's steward, and Susanna, and many others, which minister unto him of their substance" (Luke 8:3). This scripture revealed to us, the people who cared for the needs of our Lord Jesus Christ during his earthly ministry. The glory in you, if developed and utilized, will always make provision for your needs; for your vision, and your personal needs.

The glory in your life is invested into you by God so that he can get praises in return. When people shower praises on you, give glory to God. When people devote their time and efforts to support your vision, give glory to God. When you are admired by people, give glory to God. When people submit to you willingly, give glory to God. When people do their best to protect you, give glory to God. When people show you care, give glory to God. It is not by your power nor might that you enjoy these privileges. It is the Lord's doing. God cannot share his glory with anyone, make it a habit to always praise God. Just like a businessman, God invested glory in you, so that he can get more glory in return. When many people give glory to God because of you, he gets more glory in return.

2

GLORY IS OF DIFFERENT KINDS

"There is one, the glory of the sun, another of the moon, and another of the stars: a star differs from another star in glory" (1 Corinthians 15:41). This scripture says, "for one star is different from another in glory..." that is to say, glory are of different kinds.

Our God loves varieties, he created everything differently, and in varieties. For instance, there are about seven thousand five hundred varieties of apples in existence. There are about four thousand six hundred and seventy-five lizard species. Research shows that there are about twenty-one recognized human species in the world. All these, are proofs that God is a lover of varieties.

God gave different glory to different people because he wants us to shine and impact the world differently. We are to shine according to the glory that God has given each of us. Don't try to be someone else, be what God has said you should be. Trying to be like another person will destroy your genius. By so doing, you will deny the world the opportunity of benefiting from your genius. The problem with some people today is, that they are trying to be like another person. In trying to be someone else, the best you can be is *second* to that person. You can't be better than him/her, because that is not what God created you to be.

You are uniquely created, no one is exactly like you in the whole world. We are told, that the thumbprint of the Earth's population (8.1 billion people) is different from each other, no one is exactly like the other.

What field are you called to shine forth your glory. Remain there, don't derail, your field of calling may not be popular, God sent you there to make it popular. Your field of calling may not be lucrative, God sent you there to make it lucrative. Remain in your calling, that's where you are relevant and that is where your glory will shine.

God created you to be unique, so be different and stand out, that is the only way you can be recognized and celebrated in your generation.

3

LEVELS OF GLORY

"But we all, with open face beholding as in a glass the glory of the Lord, are changed into the same image from glory to glory, even as by the Spirit of the Lord" (2 Corinthians 3:18). This scripture confirmed to us that, the glory of the Lord is from one level to another, and this glory experiences exponential growth. God established hierarchies in all his kingdoms. As it is in heaven, so it is on earth.

We all are not on the same level, the level of the superior is higher than that of the inferior. So also it is with glory. The will of God for us is to graduate from one level of glory to another. As you move from one level of glory to another higher level of glory, your light will shine brighter and brighter and you will do greater exploits.

For you to discover, develop and utilize your innate glory, you must look at these three directions:

1. LOOK WITHIN: God has deposited glory inside you, you came with glory into this world. It is *called innate glory,* meaning inborn glory. It has been in you since you were born, it is your responsibility to look inward and know the kind of glory placed in you by the Creator. Until you look inward, you cannot discover who you are. There are talents God has deposited in you through which your glory will shine. Ask yourself these questions: what talent or talents, have I noticed in me that can be of benefit to others? What is it that when I watch others do, I feel that I can do better? What do people appreciate in me? What is it that other people struggle with, that I do with ease? The answers to these questions can help you discover your God's given talents. There is no man without a natural gift, you must have at least one, others have more than one. "And unto one he gave five talents, to another two, and unto another one; to every man according to his several abilities…" (Matthew 25:15). Don't neglect your gifts, if you do, you will suffer. For you to shine, you must first, discover the glory within you.

2. LOOK AROUND: For you to develop the glory within, and make it shine, you need to look around for some special kind of people, who will help you fulfill your glory. You need to look out for a mentor and glory helpers. A mentor is a wise and trusted counselor, or a teacher, who has knowledge and experience in the area of your interest. He will teach and guide you, on how to develop your potentials and put it to use. The light of your mentor or mentors will help your's shine brighter. We will talk more about mentors, later in this book. You also need to look around for glory helpers. These are people who will support and help you realize your glory. This group of people will support you with their skills, resources, and time. We all need vision helpers for our glory to be fulfilled.

3. LOOKUP: The third, and the most important direction you must look at, is to look up to God. This is because he is the one who deposited the glory in you. He knows your future and your mission in this world. He can guide, direct and empower you to fulfill your glory. You cannot succeed without God, you need his help and guidance to the top. Anytime you are confused, look up and ask him for help and guidance. "I will lift my eyes unto the hills, from whence cometh my help. My help cometh from the LORD, which made heaven and earth. He will not suffer thy foot to be moved: he that keepeth thee will not slumber" (Psalm 121:1-3). There are people with alluring glory, yet they are not seen by others. If the glory from above rises upon you, the world will see you and give you attention. "Arise, shine, for thy light is come, and the glory of the Lord is risen thee" (Isaiah 60:1). The glory of the Lord from above will make your glory visible for the world to see. If you want to shine, look unto God. "They looked unto Him and were lightened: and their faces were not ashamed" (Psalm 34:5).

FOR YOU TO MOVE FROM ONE LEVEL OF GLORY TO ANOTHER, YOU MUST BE UNVEILED

"But their minds were blinded: for until this day remaineth the same veil untaken away in the reading of the old testament; which veil is done away in Christ" (2 Corinthians 3:14).

A veil is a thing that covers or hides something from view. You cannnot see beyond a spiritual veil, it is this veil that separates one level of glory from another. For instance, it is custom in some Church's wedding services, that the bride walks into the Church building with her face covered with a veil and after the pronouncement of marriage, she's unveiled to a new level of glory. She is no longer a spinster but a married woman. From that moment, she will be accorded the honor of a married woman. So also it is in the spiritual realm, each time you are unveiled, you will step into a new level of glory, and you will see the glory, the veil of your previous level prevented you from seeing. God plans to transform us from glory to glory, that was why Jesus came into the world. Some of the Jews chose to remain in the glory of the ministration of Moses. Their minds grew callous. They lost the power of understanding, because of the veil. "But even unto this day, when Moses is read, the veil is upon their heart" (2 Corinthians 3:15). The only way to escape this level is to turn to Jesus. "Nevertheless when ye shall turn to the Lord, the veil shall be taken away" (2 Corinthians 3:16).

4

VEILS THAT HINDER PEOPLE FROM MOVING INTO GREATER GLORY

1. THE VEIL OF SIN: Sin, transgression against the law of God. If you are not living your life by the laws and will of God, you are a sinner. In 1 John 5:17: the Bible says "All unrighteousness is sin..." some of us live in partial obedience and we claim to be holy.

Some years ago, I was working as a sales supervisor in one establishment. When I came in newly, some people advised that I should join hands with them, so we can steal from the company. As a child of God, I rejected that offer. Later, we began to experience shortages in our accounts. This consistent shortage led to a reduction in our salaries, this continued for a few months. As a result of this, I stopped paying my tithes. Then one day, I saw a vision, in that vision, three young ladies stood before me. They threatened to afflict me with their powers. I asked, what my offense was, they said I'm a thief, and I don't pay tithes, this is the reason they were permitted to deal with me. Then that vision was withdrawn from me. The next month, there were shortages again, but I paid my tithe. About two days later, with the help of someone, I caught one of my sales girls stealing money. That ended the problem of shortages I have been facing. It happened because I obeyed the commandments of God by paying my tithe. I thought I was living a righteous life, but I was robbing God, of what belongs to him. That opened doors for problems to come in. To close the door of problems, avoid sin. Sin will put a veil on you, and that will prevent you from seeing the glory of God. "But your iniquities have separated between you and your God, and your sins have hidden his face from you, that he will not hear" (Isaiah 59:2).

2. THE VEIL OF UNBELIEF: Unbelief is the inability to have faith in God. We need faith to walk with God, you cannot be a genuine believer without faith. The Bible says in Hebrew 11:6: "But without faith, it is impossible to please him…" To see the glory of God, you must believe. "And Jesus said unto her, Said I not unto thee, that if thou wouldest believe, thou shouldest see the glory of God?" (John 11:40). The veil of unbelief, always prevents its victims, from seeing the glory of God. In the above scripture, after Martha believed the Lord. She saw the glory of God, her dead brother, Lazarus came back to life. (John 11:40-44). Some years back, I attended an interview, it was a written test, we were told to come back for the results of the test, a few days later. On the day of the results collection, I got there and found out that my name was not among the successful candidates. I left disappointed, on my way home, the Lord spoke to me and asked me what happened. I answered, LORD you know all things, my name was not among the successful candidates. Then the Lord spoke to me that whatever you say at home will happen to you. It was difficult to believe, but I chose to believe him. When I got home, I told everyone that I passed the interview. A few days later, I received a phone call from the company that I passed the interview. I later got that job, because I believed the Lord. I spoke the language of faith and *NO*, turned to *YES*. Believe, and you will see the glory of God.

3. THE VEIL OF IGNORANCE: Ignorance is a lack of knowledge or information. Ignorance darkens the understanding of its victims. "Having their understanding darkened, being alienated from the life of God through the ignorance that is in them, because of the blindness of their heart" (Ephesians 4:18). The blindness of their heart, in the above scripture, means that their hearts have been covered with the veil of ignorance. That is what ignorance can do to the hearts of people. Let us see how the veil of ignorance was removed from the Ethiopian eunuch in Acts 8:27-35: "And he arose and went: and behold, a man of Ethiopia, a eunuch of great authority under Candace queen of the Ethiopians, who had the charge of all her treasure, and had come to Jerusalem for worship, was returning and sitting in his chariot read Esaias the prophet. Then the Spirit said unto Philip, Go near, and join thyself to this chariot. And Philip ran thither to him, and heard him read the prophet Esaias, and said, Understandest thou what thou readest? And he said, How can I, except some man guide me? And he desired Philip that he would come up and sit with him. The place of the scripture which he read was this, "He was lead as a sheep to the slaughter; and like a lamb dumb before his shearer, so opened he, not his mouth: In his humiliation, his judgment was taken away:

and who shall declare his generation? For his life is taken from the earth". And the eunuch answered Philip, and said, I pray thee, of whom speaketh the prophet this? Of himself, or some other man? Then Philip opened his mouth, and began at the same scripture, and preached unto him, Jesus." This Ethiopian eunuch was a proselyte of Judaism, the religion of the Jews. He was ignorant of the gospel of Jesus, so the Holy Spirit sent Philip to remove the veil of ignorance by the preaching of the gospel. Each time a man is about to be promoted to the next level, the veil of ignorance of the new level will be removed from him. Once the veil of ignorance is unveiled, you will see and step into the glory of the next level.

4. VEIL OF FAILURES: Failure is a lack of success. When failure is experienced repeatedly, it makes the mind weary and discouraged, such mind is veiled, and will not be able to see the glory of success. "And he entered into one of the ships, which Simon's, and prayed him that he would thrust out a little from the land. And he sat down and taught the people out of the ship. Now when he had left speaking, he said unto Simon, Launch out into the deep, and let down your nets for a draught. And Simon answering said unto him, Master, we have toiled all night, and have taken nothing: nevertheless, at thy word, I will let down the net. And when they had this done, they inclosed a great multitude of fishes: and their net broke" (Luke 5:3-6). Peter had toiled all night, yet he could not catch any fish. The veil of the failure experienced prevented him from trying again. He was preparing to go home when Jesus step into the situation. Jesus used the ship of Peter to preach to the people. When he had finished speaking, he told Peter to throw his net into the lake, so that he can catch fish. Peter obeyed, and he caught a multitude of fish. Jesus removed the veil of past failure from Peter and he saw the glory of God. The veil of past failures can prevent people from seeing the glory of the next level. That is why you don't need to give up, keep trying, remain in prayer, and in no time you will see the glory of success. It takes courage to get this veil removed, it is a veil that has prevented many people from moving into glory.

5. VEIL OF TRADITION AND DOCTRINE:

Tradition is an inherited, established, or customary pattern of thought, action, or behavior. While the doctrine is a belief or set of beliefs, held and taught by a church, or other groups. There are some tradition and doctrines, that prevents people from seeing the glory of the next level. Let's take for example in Acts 10:9-16: "On the morrow, as they went on their journey, and drew nigh unto the city, Peter went up upon the housetop to pray about the sixth hour: And he became very hungry, and would have eaten: but while they made ready, he fell into a trance and saw heaven opened, and a certain vessel descending unto him, as it had been a great sheet knit at the four corners, and let down to the earth: Wherein were all manner of four-footed beasts of the earth, wild beasts, creeping things, and fowls of the air. And there came a voice to him, Rise, Peter; kill, and eat. But Peter said, Not so Lord; for I have never eaten anything common or unclean. And the voice spake unto him again the second time, What God hath cleansed, that call not thou common. This was done thrice: and the vessel was received up again into heaven." The Jews according to their tradition, don't eat unclean animals and they don't keep company with the Gentiles. God was about to send Peter to the house of Cornelius a Gentile, to preach the gospel of Jesus to his household. So God lifted the standard and suspended the Jews tradition for Peter so that he can reach the Gentiles. It is important to know that God can overrule any tradition or doctrine of men. He can lift the standard for you so that you will see a higher glory. He is the Sovereign LORD of the universe. No one can question him. Some years ago, I was invited to minister in a church vigil meeting, I had planned to fast in line with tradition, but the Lord told me not to fast, he said, I should just pray and study the word of God. I obeyed reluctantly, to my surprise, the power of God moved in that meeting in a way, I have never seen before, those in attendance received the touch of God. The instructions of God are more important than any human tradition and doctrines.

6. VEIL OF WORLDLINESS: To be worldly is to be concerned with material values or ordinary life rather than a spiritual existence. If your mind is controlled mainly, by the thoughts of material things and ordinary things of this world then you are a worldly person. To be worldly is to be carnally minded. "Because the carnal mind is enmity against God: for it is not subject to the law of God, neither indeed can be" (Romans 8:7). The care of the things of this world, if not checked, can turn a man completely away from God. Apostle Paul wrote in (2Timothy 4:10) "For Demas hath forsaken me, having loved this present world..." Be careful, don't give too much attention to material and ordinary affairs of this world. "But seek ye first the kingdom of God and his righteousness, and all these things shall be added unto you" (Matthew 6:33). We are to seek first the kingdom of God, the thoughts and pursuit of the things of this world have taken some people away from the presence of God. They no longer have time to pray and to study the word of God. Some don't even attend church services anymore. This is not supposed to be so. Whatever blessing takes you away from the presence of God is not from God. God will not give you what will destroy you, beware! If you serve God faithfully, he will bless you in return. Be careful, don't let love for material things control your mind, it will put a veil on your heart and prevent you from seeing the glory of God. "If riches increase, set not your heart upon them" (Psalm 62:10). Whatever controls your heart will control the whole of your life. Prosperity in itself is not bad, however, don't let the thoughts of material acquisition control your mind. You need to create time for your spiritual development. It is in doing this that you can be transformed from glory to glory.

5

DIMENSIONS OF GLORY

Glory is in different dimensions, to gain clarity on the dimensions of glory, we will be discussing the dimensions one after the other.

1. GLORY AS POWER: Power is the ability to do or undergo something. It is also the capacity or ability to direct and influence the behavior of others or the course of events. "God hath spoken once; twice have I heard this; that power belongeth unto God" (Psalm 62:11). Power belongs to God, he is the one who gives power to people. Power is glorious, power puts you in charge. Spiritual power is the greatest of all powers. God gives power to people so that they can use it to help others. By so doing, the world will become a better place. Whatever power that God has given you, use it to serve others. "How God anointed Jesus of Nazareth with the Holy Ghost and with power: who went about doing good and healing all that were oppressed of the devil; for God was with him" (Acts 10:38). Our Lord Jesus understood the purpose of power, he used it to serve the people and God was pleased with him. Don't use power to oppress other people, that is not the reason why God gave it to you. If you want God to be with you, as he was with Jesus, use your power for the good of all, not for selfish purposes.

2. GLORY AS BEAUTY: Beauty is the quality of being attractive, pleasing, fine, or good-looking. It also means, the quality present in a thing or person that makes it give intense pleasure or deep satisfaction to the mind. All beauty comes from God. He is the one who gives beauty to people according to his wish. "And let the beauty of the Lord our God be upon us..." (Psalm 90:17). The main reason why God beautifies people is for his name to be praised. When people appreciate your beauty, give the praises back to God. You are not the one who created yourself, it was God who created you and made you beautiful. He also gave you those beautiful qualities, that people observe in you. "But in all Israel, there was none praised as Absalom for his beauty: from the sole of his foot even to the crown of his head there was no blemish in him" (2 Samuel 14:25). People praised Absalom for his beauty. This is because beauty generates praises, and all praises must be returned to God. Failure to return God's glory to him can lead to severe punishment. God can beautify you in many ways, he can beautify your appearance, he can beautify your career, he can beautify your marriage, he can beautify your ministry, and many more.

3. GLORY AS GREATNESS: To be great is to have the ability, quality, or eminence considerably above average. It is God that makes people great. No one can make himself great, without the support of God. "For by strength shall no man prevail" (1 Samuel 2:9). Through this scripture, we can see that the strength of man alone cannot make him great. God can raise someone from the dust and make him into a great person. He can overthrow another, he is the Sovereign LORD! He can take you from one degree of greatness to the other. "Thou shalt increase my greatness and comfort me on every side" (Psalm 71:21). He raised Abraham and made him great beyond his imagination. "And I will make of thee a great nation, and I will bless thee, and make thy name great, and thou shalt be a blessing" (Genesis 12:2). God increased the greatness of

Abraham until he became a blessing to the whole world. He can do the same for you if you are willing and obedient.

4. GLORY AS HONOR: Honor is high respect, great esteem, or value. It is also the quality of knowing and doing what is morally right. God is the most honorable personality in the universe. It is he who gives honor to those who please him. "Glory and honor are in his presence; strength and gladness are in his place" (1 Chronicles 16:27). "Riches and honor are with me..." (Proverbs 8:18). God raised Jabez from the position of dishonor to the position of honor. "And Jabez was more honorable than his brethren: and his mother called his name Jabez saying Because I bare him with sorrow. And Jabez called on the God of Israel, saying, Oh, that thou wouldest bless me indeed, and enlarge my coast, and that thine hand might be with me, and that thou wouldest keep me from evil, that it may not grieve me! And God granted him that which he requested" (1 Chronicle 4:9-10). If God raises and honor you, you must be thoughtful to always return honor to him. "Wherefore the LORD God of Israel saith, I said indeed that thy house, and the house of thy father, should walk before me forever: but now the LORD saith, Be it far from me; for them that honor me I will honor, and they that despise me shall be lightly esteemed" (1 Samuel 2:30). The family of Eli failed to honor God because of their sinful lifestyle, and God removed them from the position of honor. Honor is from God, and it must be returned to Him.

5. GLORY AS DIGNITY: Dignity is the quality or state of being worthy, honored, or esteemed. Treating people with dignity implies treating them with courtesy and kindness, it also means, respecting their rights. The difference between honor and dignity is that honor cultures place importance on socially conferred worth, reputation, and a positive social image, all of which can be granted or taken away by others. In contrast, dignity cultures place importance on context-independent, individual, and inherent worth, which is less affected by the social regard of others. Dignity is of God, that is why we honor and esteem him for who he is. It is he who invests dignity in people. If you are a man of dignity, you are a man of glory. "And one Ananias, a devout man according to the law, having a good report of all the Jews which dwelt there" (Acts 22:12). To have a good report is to have dignity. Ananias was a man of dignity. As a result of the good qualities he possessed, the Jews honored and esteemed him. "And they said, Cornelius the centurion, a just man and one that feareth God, and of good report among all the nation of the Jews..." (Acts 10:22). Cornelius was also a man of dignity, because of his *just* lifestyle and the Bible recorded that he feared the Lord.

6. GLORY AS EXCELLENCE: Excellence is the quality of being outstanding. Excellence is of God, it is he who gives the spirit of excellence to people. "Touching the Almighty, we cannot find him out: he is excellent in power, and in judgment, and plenty of Justice..." (Job 37:23). "Thou art more glorious and excellent than the mountains of prey" (Psalm 76:4). "Let them praise the name of the Lord: for his name alone is excellent..." (Psalm 148:13). The Lord our God is the most excellent one. He gave David the spirit of excellence, and he excelled than all the presidents and princes, in the land of Babylon. "Daniel was preferred above the presidents and princes because an excellent spirit was in him, and the king thought to set him over the whole realm" (Daniel 6:3). When the spirit of excellence is in a man, he will surpass the records of others. Everywhere he goes, he will be preferred above others. Such a person will experience rapid promotion. He will be highly favored. The spirit of excellence in the spirit of virtue.

7. GLORY AS WISDOM: Wisdom is the quality of having experience, knowledge, and good judgment. To be wise is to be sensible and prudent. God is the wisest, only he is. "Now unto the King eternal, immortal, invisible, the only wise God, be honor and glory forever and ever Amen" (1 Timothy 1:17). "Daniel answered and said, Blessed, be the name of God forever and ever: for wisdom and might are his" (Daniel 2:20). God is the one who gives wisdom, if you want wisdom, ask him. "If anyone lack wisdom, let him ask of God, that giveth to all men liberally, and upbraideth not, and it shall be given him" (James 1:5). The wisdom of God in Joseph, made him become a ruler in the land of Egypt. "And Pharaoh said unto Joseph, Forasmuch as God hath shewed thee all this, there is none so discreet and wise as thou art. Thou shall be over my house, and according to unto thy word shall all my people be ruled: only in the throne will I be greater than thou" (Genesis 41:39-40). The wisdom of God in Daniel made him excel in the land of Babylon. "Then the king made Daniel a great man, and gave him lots of great gifts, and made him ruler over the whole province of Babylon, and chief of the governors over all the wise men of Babylon" (Daniel 2:48). Through the wisdom of God, Solomon excelled above all the kings of the earth in his days. "And all the kings of the earth sought the presence of Solomon, to hear his wisdom, that God had put in his heart" (2 Chronicles 9:23).

8. GLORY AS AUTHORITY: Authority is the power or right to give orders, make decisions, and enforce obedience. It also means the power you exercise on behalf of another person. God is the source of all authority, and he gives it to people either directly or indirectly. He can put someone in the position of authority, and he can remove a fellow from such a position if he likes. "And he changeth the times and seasons: he removeth kings, and setteth up kings..." (Daniel 2:21). God puts people in the office so that they can use their good office to serve the people and make life better for them. Authority is not to be used for selfish purposes. "When the righteous are in authority the people rejoice: but when the wicked beareth rule, the people mourn" (Proverbs 29:2). God gave authority to Jesus and he used it for the good of all "And they were all amazed, to an extent that they questioned among themselves, saying, what thing is this? For with authority commandeth he even the unclean spirits, and they obey him" (Mark 1:27). Whatever the authority God has given you, use it for the good of all. So that through your service, people will give glory to God.

9. GLORY AS HOLINESS: God is the holiest, he is so holy that his eyes cannot behold iniquities. To be holy is to be perfect or flawless. "And one cried unto another, and said, Holy, holy, holy, is the Lord of hosts: the whole earth is full of his glory" (Isaiah 6:3). His angels are holy. "When the son of man shall come in his glory, and all the holy angels with him..." (Matthew 25:31). God's dwelling place is holy, and wherever he steps on becomes holy ground. "And when the Lord saw that he turned aside to see, God called unto him out of the midst of the bush, and said, Moses, Moses, And he said, "Here am I". And he said, Draw not nigh hither: put off thy shoes from off thy feet, for the place whereon thou standest is holy ground" (Exodus 3:4-5). God expects all his children to be holy. "Be ye therefore perfect, even as your Father which is in heaven is perfect" (Matthew 5:48). Perfection is a lifetime journey, but we must make efforts to work towards it daily.

10. GLORY AS LIGHT: Light is the opposite of darkness. It could also be defined as the natural agent that stimulates sight and makes things visible. God is light, it is he that gives light to everyone and everything that shines. "This then is the message which we have heard of him, and declare unto you, that God is light, and in him is no darkness at all" (1 John 1:5). "Who only hath immortality, dwelling in the light which no man can approach unto; whom no man hath seen, nor can see: to whom be honor and power everlasting. Amen" (1 Timothy 6:16). In the kingdom of God, the greater the glory, the greater the light. This applies to both angels and men. "And was transfigured before them: and his face did shine as the sun, and his raiment was white as the light" (Matthew 17:2). "And lo, the angel of the Lord came upon them, and the glory of the Lord shonaroundnd them: and they were so afraid" (Luke 2:9). Every genuine child of God is light, their duty is to shine in this dark world. "Ye are the light of the world. A city that is set on a hill cannot be hidden. Neither do men light a candle and put it under a bushel, but on a candlestick; and it giveth light unto all that are in the house. Let your light so shine before men, that they may see your good works, and glorify you Father which is in heaven" (Matthew 5:14-16). The little light that was in you, when you gave your life to Jesus is expected to shine brighter and brighter forever. "But the path of the just is as a shining light, that shineth more and more unto the perfect day" (Proverbs 4:18). To shine means, to do good work, and to shine brighter is to increase in good works.

6

FOUR MAJOR LEVELS OF GLORY FOR BELIEVERS

1. THE GLORY OF A CHILD OF GOD: Real glory begins when you give your life to Jesus and invite him to be your Lord and savior. There is no glory in being a servant of the devil. The day you give your life to Jesus, you receive the glory of an overcomer. "For whatsoever is born of God overcometh the world: and this is the victory that overcometh, even our faith. Who is he that overcometh the world, but he that believeth that Jesus is the Son of God" (1 John 5:4-5). On the day you gave your life to Jesus, you became a child of light. "While ye have light, believe in the light, that ye may be children of light..." (John 12:36). "Who hath delivered us from the power of darkness, and hath translated us into the kingdom of his dear Son" (Colossians 1:13). The children of God at this level, are fed with the milk of the word of God. "As newborn babes, desire the sincere milk of the word, that ye may grow thereby" (1 Peter 2:2). "For everyone that useth milk is unskillful in the word of righteousness: for he is a babe" (Hebrew 5:13).

2. THE GLORY OF A SON OF GOD: A son is a matured believer, who is skillful in the word of God. He has grown from baby level to become a son. Unlike babes, he feeds on the meat level of the word of God. Milk is for babes while meat is for sons. "But strong meat belongeth to them that are of full age, even those who by reason of use have their senses exercised to discern both good and evil" (Hebrews 5:14). The sons of God, are those believers who have developed their relationship with God, to the extent that they and God communicate often. They are filled with the spirit, and they are always led by the spirit. "For as many as are led by the spirit of God, they are the sons of God" (Romans 8:14). "And because ye are sons, God hath sent forth the spirit of his Son into your hearts, crying, Abba, Father" (Galatians 4:6). Sons of God ought to be perfect and flawless in their dealings with others. "That ye may be blameless and harmless, the sons of God, without rebuke, Amid, crooked and perverse nation, among whom ye shine as lights in the world" (Philippians 2:15). Sons must go through trials to be tested. "Though he were a Son, yet learned he obedience by the things which he suffered" (Hebrews 5:8). "Behold, I have refined thee, but not with silver; I have chosen thee in the furnace of affliction" (Isaiah 48:10).

3. GLORY OF A STAR OF GOD: The stars of God, are the servants of God, who assist him in governing the nations of the earth. Each star of God is appointed over a nation. "But I will show thee that which is noted in the scripture of truth: and there is none that holdeth with me in these things, but Michael your prince" (Daniel 10:2). Angel Michael is the star of God, that was appointed over the nation of Israel. The office of the star of God is for both angels and men, who have grown from the level of sons to the level of servants of God. The prophet Samuel was a star of God, he was a prophet over the whole nation of Israel. "And Samuel spoke unto all the house of Israel, saying, if ye do return unto the Lord with all your hearts, then put away the strange god's and Ashtaroth from among you, and prepare your hearts unto the Lord, and serve him only: and he will deliver you out of the hand of the Philistines" (1 Samuel 7:3). The duties of the star of God, are to guide, direct, lead and protect, the nation assigned to him by God. "Behold, I send an angel before thee, to keep thee in thy way, and to bring thee into the place which I have prepared. Beware of him, and obey his voice, provoke him not; for he will not pardon your transgression: for my name is in him. But if thou shalt indeed obey his voice, and do all that I speak; then I will be an enemy unto thine enemies, and an adversary unto thine adversaries. For mine, Angel shall go before thee, and bring thee in unto the Amorites, and the Hittites, and the Perizzites, and the Jebusites: and I will cut them off" (Exodus 23:20-23). We saw in this scripture, that the star of God is the representative of God and a ruler over his God's given nation. Through the authority of the office of Prophet Samuel, as the star of God. The nation of Israel was protected from its enemies all the days of Samuel. "So the Philistines were subdued, and they came no more into the coast of Israel: and the hand of the Lord was against the Philistines all the days of Samuel" (1 Samuel 7:13).

4. GLORY OF THE MORNING STAR: The morning star is chief among the stars of God, his duty is to assist God to govern the nations assigned to him. The difference between the assignment of the star of God and the morning star is that the star of God oversees one nation, while the morning star oversees many nations. Our Lord Jesus is not the only morning star in the Bible. "When the morning star sang together, and all the sons of God shouted for joy" (Job 38:7). The position of the morning star can be attained by both men and angels. "See, I have this day set thee over the nations and the kingdoms, to root out, and to pull down, and to destroy, and to throw down, to build and to plant" (Jeremiah 1:10). God set Prophet Jeremiah over nations and kingdoms. Note that nations and kingdoms were in plural form. So, Jeremiah was placed in the office of the morning star. The morning star rules the nations with a rod of iron. "Thou shalt break them with a rod of iron: thou shalt dash them in pieces like a Potter's vessel" (Psalm 2:9). "And he shall rule them with a rod of iron; as the vessels of a Potter shall they be broken to shivers: even as I receive of my father" (Revelation 2:27). The rod of iron signifies the authority to root out, to pull down, to destroy, to throw down, to build, and to plant. In other words, the power to make and Mar. Every morning star, have a seat at the mount of the congregation. The mount of the congregation is the mountain where the stars of God, gather to worship and to commune with him. "For thou hast said in thine heart, I will ascend into heaven, I will exalt my throne above the stars of God: I will sit also upon the mount of the congregation, in the sides of the north" (Isaiah 14:13). "Again there was a day when the sons of God came to present themselves before the Lord, and Satan came along with them to present himself before the Lord" (Job 2:1). The Lord Jesus is the one who appoints people to the office of the morning star. "And he that overcometh, and keepeth my works unto the end, to him will I give power over the nations. And he shall rule them with a rod of iron, as the vessels of a Potter shall they be broken to shivers: even as I received of my Father. And I will give him the morning star" (Revelation 2:26-28). You can rise from the level of an ordinary human to a god over the nations. You can become the morning star! Jesus, the bright morning star has promised to give the position of the morning star, to whoever overcomes, and you can be one of them. "I, Jesus have sent my angel to testify unto you these things in the churches, I am the root and the offspring of David, the bright morning star" (Revelation 22:16).

7

THINGS TO DO, TO MOVE FROM GLORY TO GLORY

1. GIVE YOUR LIFE TO JESUS: Real glory begins when you accept Jesus as your Lord and savior. From that moment you have become a child of God. The devil and his agents do not have power over you anymore. You have become a citizen of the kingdom of God. "Jesus answered and said unto him, verily, verily, I say unto thee, Except a man be born again, he can not see the kingdom of God" (John 3:3). For you to be saved, you need to confess Jesus as your Lord and savior with your mouth. "For with the heart man believeth unto righteousness; and with the mouth, confession is made unto salvation" (Romans 10:10). When a sinner turns to the Lord in repentance. The Lord will remove the veil of sin from him and he will be ushered into the glory of being a child of God. Whenever a veil is removed from someone, such arson can see greater glory and step into it. If you have not given your life to Jesus, you have the opportunity to do so now. If you want to give your life to Jesus, please pray this prayer aloud: Lord Jesus I come to you today as a sinner, please forgive my sins, and wash me in your blood. I confess you as my Lord and personal savior today, come into my life and dwell in me forever. I surrender my life to you completely. Thank you for accepting me into your kingdom. In Jesus' mighty name I have prayed.

Congratulations you are now a child of God, welcome to God's kingdom!

2. STUDY THE BIBLE DAILY: The Bible is the word of God, it is the Creator's manual for our lives, it was written to guide, correct, and instruct us. "All scripture is given by the inspiration of God and is profitable for doctrine, for reproof, for correction, for instruction in righteousness" (2 Timothy 3:16). For you to experience success, you need to study the word of God daily. We are in a generation where some people don't have time to study the Bible anymore. They spend most of their time on social media doing nothing and achieving nothing. Some are looking for success the wrong way. The most reliable source of success is the word of God. "This book of the law shall not depart out of thy mouth; but thou shalt meditate therein day and night, that thou mayest observe to do according to all that is written therein; for then thou shalt make thy way prosperous, and then thou shalt have success" (Joshua 1:8). The word of God is the sword of the spirit, that we use to fight spiritual battles to conquer the enemy. When you are in a battle with the enemies, you need to quote the word of God to defeat them. Jesus defeated the devil when he came to tempt him, not with prayer alone, but also with the word of God. If you don't study the Bible, you will not have the sword of the spirit to fight the enemies. "And when the tempter came to him, he said, if thou be the son of God, command that these stones be made bread. But he answered and said, it is written, Man shall not live by bread alone, but by every word that proceedeth out of the mount of God" (Matthew 4:3). "And take the helmet of salvation, and the sword of the spirit, which is the word of God" (Ephesians 6:17). As you study the word of God daily, and you obey the instructions in it. Continuously, the light of the glory of God will increase in your heart, until the light of Christ is fully shining in you. When you get to this spiritual level, you will shine brighter like the sun of righteousness. "We have also, a more sure word of prophecy; whereunto ye do well that ye take heed, as unto a light that shineth in a dark place, until the day dawn, and the day star arise in your hearts" (2 Peter 1:19). "And was transfigured before them: and his face did shine as the sun, and his raiment was white as the light" (Matthew 17:2).

3. PRAY OFTEN: Praying is the process of talking to God. We pray to God, to praise him and to make our requests known unto him. Prayer gives us access to fellowship with God. Every believer must have a healthy prayer life. Our Lord Jesus lived a life of prayer. "And in the morning, rising a great while before day, he went out and departed into a solitary place, and there prayed" (Mark 1:35). "And he withdrew himself into the wilderness and prayed" (Luke 5:16). Prayer promotes spiritual growth and empowers the believer who prays always. A man of prayer is a man of power, and a man of power is a man of miracles. "Now there was at Joppa a certain disciple named Tabitha, which by interpretation is called Dorcas: this woman was full of good works and almsgiving. And it came to pass in those days, that she was sick, and died:

whom when they had washed, they laid her in an upper chamber. And forasmuch, as Lydda was nigh to Joppa, and the disciples had heard that Peter was there, they sent unto him two men, desiring him that he would not delay coming to them. Then Peter arose and went with them. When he came, they brought him into the upper chamber: and all the widows stood by him weeping, and showing the coats and garments which Dorcas made, while she was with them. But Peter put them all forth, and kneeled, and prayed: and turning him to the body said, Tabitha, arise. And she opened her eyes: and when she saw Peter, she sat up. And he gave her his hand and lifted hep, and when he had called the saints and widows, presented her alive" (Acts 9:36). Prayer is not what you engage in two or three times daily. You are to pray often. "Pray without ceasing" (1 Thessalonians 5:17). Ask the Lord to give you the power to pray always. The more you pray, the brighter your light will shine.

4. LIVE A HOLY LIFE: To be holy is to obey God in all things. It is not to obey the written word of God alone but to also obey all the instructions given to you by the Lord. Partial obedience is not holiness, you must obey God in all things. "For whosoever shall keep the whole law, and yet offend in one point, he is guilty of all" (James 2:10). A life of holiness purifies the soul. "Seeing ye have purified your souls in obeying the truth..." (1 Peter 1:22). A purified soul is a soul with clean hands and a pure heart. This is the kind of person that will keep rising, from one level of glory to another until he can stand in God's holy place, which is the amount of the congregation. "Who shall ascend into the hill of the LORD? or who shall stand in his holy place? He that hath clean hands, and a pure heart: who hath not lifted his soul unto vanity, nor sworn deceitfully" (Psalm 24:3-4). "Blessed are the pure in heart: for they shall see God" (Matthew 5:8). To see God, to have fellowship with him, and to shine brighter and brighter, it is expedient to live a holy life always.

5. BE FAITHFUL: To be faithful is to remain loyal and steadfast. It also means, to be reliable; worthy of trust. God promotes the faithful ones, God is always looking for the faithful ones who he can promote from one level of glory to a higher level of glory. "And I will raise me a faithful priest, that shall do according to that which is in mine heart and my mind: and I will build him a sure house, and he shall walk before mine anointed forforever1 Samuel 2:35). "His lord said unto him, well done, thou good and faithful servant: thou hast been faithful over a few things, I will make thee ruler over many things: enter thou into the joy of the Lord" (Matthew 25:21). If you want your service to be rewarded, you must be faithful. "Moreover it is required in stewards, that a man be found faithful" (1 Corinthians 4:2). God raised Moses and made him great because he was a faithful man. "My servant Moses is not so, who is faithful in all My house" (Numbers 12:7). Are you loyal? Are you reliable? When you have challenges, where do you go to seek solutions? Can God trust you? Do you praise God in your period of difficulties? Can you publicly declare your faith? God promoted Daniel and his friends in the land of Babylon, because they remained faithful to God, in their challenges. (Daniel 6:4-28 / Daniel 3:1-30). If you want to move from one level of glory to another, be faithful. "And he said unto him, Well, thou good servant: because thou hast been faithful in a very little, have thou authority over ten cities" (Luke 19:17).

6. FAST REGULARLY: Fasting is abstinence from food and drink for prayer. The abstention may be complete or partial, lengthy, or short duration. Our Lord Jesus Christ fasted during his earthly ministry. "And when he had fasted forty days and forty nights, he was afterward an hungered" (Matthew 4:2). The Apostles of Jesus fasted often, it was during fasting and prayers of the Apostles, that Barnabas and Saul (Paul) received a spiritual promotion. "As they ministered to the Lord, and fasted, the Holy Ghost said, Separate me Barnabas and Saul for the work whereunto I have called them" (Acts 13:2). Through fasting and prayer, Cornelius saw the glory of the Lord. "And Cornelius said, Four days ago I was fasting until this hour, and at the ninth hour I prayed in my house, and behold a man stood before me in bright clothing. And said, Cornelius, thy prayer is heard, and thine alms are had in remembrance in the sight of God" (Acts 10:30-31). Fasting and prayer increase spiritual power. An increase in spiritual power will enable you to do more good works. That means your light will shine brighter and brighter, and you will keep rising from one level of glory to another.

7. SERVICE: The purpose of glory is to shine, to shine is to be full of good works. A light that fails to shine is without value. To serve God is to use your spiritual gifts to serve in one or more departments in your local church, and to be of benefit to people everywhere. "Let your light so shine before men, that they may see your good works, and glorify your Father which is in heaven" (Matthew 5:16). There are many believers today, who go to church just for worship. They don't belong to any department in the church. It is a sin for you not to use your talents to glorify God. "Then he which had received the one talent came and said, Lord, I knew thee that thou art a hard man, reaping where thou hast not sown, and gathering where thou hast not strawed: And I was afraid, and went and hid thy talent in the earth: lo, there thou hast that is thine. His Lord answered and said unto him, Thou wicked and slothful servant, thou knewest that I reap where I sowed not, and gather where I not strawed: Thou oughtest therefore to have put my money to the exchangers and then at my coming I should have received mine own with usury. Take therefore the talent from him, and give it unto him which hath ten talents" (Matthew 25:24-28). If you want God to bless you, then work for him. There are lots to be done, God needs your service. To be on the payroll of any company, you have to be a worker in that company. To be on God's payroll, you have to be working for him regularly. God rewards and promotes those who use their talents to work for him. "He also that had received two talents came and said, Lord, thou deliveredst unto me two talents: behold, I have gained two other talents beside them. His lord said unto him, well done, good and faithful servant; thou hast been faithful over a few things; I will make thee ruler over many things: enter thou into the joy of the Lord" (Matthew 25:23-24). "And they that be wise shall shine as the brightness of the firmament, and they that turn many to righteousness as the stars forever and ever" (Daniel 12:3). The most rewarding work you can do for God is to win souls into his kingdom. It is one of the requirements for becoming a star of God. Money is also a talent, if you have it, use it to support the work of God.

8. SEEK KNOWLEDGE: Knowledge is familiarity or understanding of a particular skill in a branch of learning. You can not acquire all the knowledge in the world, focus more on the knowledge that is related to your skills and talents. This will help you develop and utilize your skills and talents well, and you will shine. Attend workshops and seminars, enroll yourself in a school. You can also study privately. You cannot shine without knowledge, it is a terrible thing to be without knowledge. "Also, that the soul is without knowledge, it is not good…" (Proverbs 19:2). "Apply thine heart unto instruction, and thine ears to the words of knowledge" (Proverbs 23:12). Knowledge will make you prosperous. "And by knowledge shall the chambers be filled with all precious and pleasant riches" (Proverbs 24:4). Knowledge enlightens, an enlightened man shines his light on the pathways of others. "And Jesus went about all Galilee, teaching in their synagogues, and preaching the gospel of the kingdom, and healing all manner of sickness and all manner of disease among the people" (Matthew 4:23). "Paul also and Barnabas continue in Antioch, teaching and preaching the word of the Lord, with many others also" (Acts 15:35). You cannot teach without knowledge, the more you acquire knowledge the more your light will shine. That means, continuous acquisition of knowledge, will transform you from glory to glory.

9. KNOW YOUR VISION: Develop and fulfill it: vision is your God's given dream of what you are to become in life. It is the sole purpose God sent you into this world. You were created to solve a problem, there is something you can do better than others. Your vision is the reason why you are existing, hence, the only area you can shine than others, is the area of your vision. You need to know why God sent you into this world. So that you can live a meaningful life. To discover your vision, you need to seek the face of God in prayer. He is the one who created you, he alone knows the purpose (WHY) he created you. "Then the word of the Lord came unto me, saying, Before I formed thee in the belly I knew thee; and before thou camest forth out of the womb I sanctified thee and I ordained thee a prophet unto the nations" (Jeremiah 1:4-5). Some years ago, I was praying, preparing for our Bible study, then the Lord showed me a vision. I saw a young lady dressed like a lawyer, and the vision was taken away from me. Later in the evening as I was teaching in the program. A young lady walked into our midst, I recognized her as the lady, I saw in my vision, I later asked her what she was doing for a living. She said she is an undergraduate, studying accountancy. She was supposed to be a lawyer, but she was preparing to be an accountant. Many people like that young lady, have missed their real calling in life. If you are not sure about your calling, please ask the Lord. After you have discovered your vision, develop it, work on it and make it a reality, and your glory will shine for the world to see. "And his fame went throughout all Syria: and they brought unto him all sick people that were taken with divers diseases and torments, and those which were possessed with devils, and those which were lunatic and those that had the palsy: and he healed them. And there followed him great multitudes of people from Galilee, and Decapolis, and Jerusalem, and Judaea, and from beyond Jordan" (Matthew 4:24-25).

10. BE A GIVER: A giver is someone who gives to support the work of God or to support the needy. Giving open doors for blessings and promotion. As you give, you will receive it back in multiple-fold. It can also return to you in another form of blessing. King Solomon gave to God a thousand burnt offerings, and the Lord gave him wisdom and understanding. The Lord also blessed him with great riches. All these happened, just because he gave something big to God (1 Kings 3:4-13). If you want to be blessed, cultivate the habit of giving. When you give, you will receive it back in multiple folds. "Give, and it shall be given unto you: good measure, pressed down, and shaken together, and running over, shall men give into your bosom. For with the same measure that ye mete withal it shall be measured to you again" (Luke 6:38). It is not only money that you can give to God. You can give your material possessions to God. You can also give your time and services to his work. Don't say, I don't have anything, there is something you have that you can't give. Tithes and offerings are parts of giving. If you want to be blessed, give your tithes and offerings faithfully. Some years ago, a man came to us for counseling, he explained how he has been moving from one problem to the other. The Lord said I should ask him if he's paying his tithes, I asked and he said no, I prayed with him and instructed him to go and begin tithing. He obeyed, and his life became better again. Another sister called us on phone, she explained how she has been spending money on sickness and different challenges. I asked if she has been paying her tithes, she said she doesn't pay tithes. I advised that she should begin to pay her tithes, she obeyed and the Lord stopped the activities of the devourers in her life. "Bring ye all the tithes into the storehouse, that there may be meat in my house, and prove me now herewith, saith the LORD of hosts, If I will not open you the windows of heaven, and pour you out a blessing, that there shall not be room enough to receive it" (Malachi 3:10). Apart from giving to God, it is also important that you give to the needy. "Blessed is he that considereth the poor: the Lord will deliver him in time of trouble. The Lord will preserve him, and keep him alive: and he shall be blessed upon the earth: and thou wilt not deliver him unto the will of his enemies" (Psalm 41:1-2). "But when thou makest a feast, call the poor, the maimed, the lame, the blind: And thou shalt be blessed: for they cannot recompense thee: for thou shalt be recompensed at the resurrection of the just" (Luke 14:13-14).

11. BE HONEST: To be honest is to be free of deceit, to be truthful and sincere. An honest man will always tell the truth. Such a man is not given to swindling, lying, or fraud. Wealth acquired through fraud will not last long. "Wealth gotten by vanity shall be diminished: but he that gathereth by labor shall increase" (Proverbs 13:11).

The Bible instructs that we should be honest in all our conversations. "Having your conversation honest among the Gentiles: that whereas they speak against you as evildoers, they may by your good works, which they shall behold, glorify God in the day of visitation. If you have an honest heart, you will be fruitful in everything you do, and God will bless the works of your hands. "But that on the good ground are they, which in an honest and good heart, having heard the word, keep it, and bring forth fruit with patience" (Luke 8:15). If you are honest, God will promote you in due season, it may take some time, but you will surely get to the top. We have heard the testimony of a messenger that was promoted to the post of manager because he was an honest man. People are always willing to promote and relate with an honest man. "Wherefore, brethren, look ye out among you seven men of honest report, full of the Holy Ghost and wisdom, whom we may appoint over this business. But we will give ourselves continually to prayer, and the ministry of the word. And the saying pleased the whole multitude: and they chose Stephen, a man full of faith and the Holy Ghost, and Philip, and Prochorus and Nicanor and Timon, and

Parmenas, and Nicolas a proselyte of Antioch, whom they set before the apostles: and when they had prayed, they laid their hands on them" (Acts 6:3-6). One of the qualities that were found in these men, that were promoted in the quoted scripture, was that they were all honest men. When you live an honest life, you will shine wherever you are located.

12. BE DILIGENT: To be diligent is to be hardworking and focused. God the Father and our Lord Jesus are diligent workers. "But Jesus answered them, My Father worketh hitherto, and I work" (John 5:17). For you to be transformed from glory to glory, you need to work hard and be very focused. There are lots of distractions in the world today that can make you lose focus. Be focused and work hard to achieve your vision. Hard work promotes, laziness demotes. A lazy man will suffer hunger and poverty. His soul will desire good things but he will not be able to get them. "Slothfulness casteth into a deep sleep, and an idle soul shall suffer hunger" (Proverbs 19:15). "The desire of the slothful killeth him: for his hands refuse to labor" (Proverbs 21:25). "I went by the field of the slothful, and by the vineyard of the man void of understanding. And, lo, it was all grown over with thorns, and nettles had covered the face thereof, and the stone wall thereof, was broken down" (Proverbs 24:30-31). The diligent man will rule over lazy men. "The hand of the diligent shall bear rule: but the slothful shall be under tribute" (Proverbs 12:24). Diligence will bring a man into greatness. He will have the privilege of relating with the higher-ups in his society. "Seest thou a man diligent in his business? He shall stand before kings; he shall not stand before mean men" (Proverbs 22:29). If you want to move from glory to glory, be diligent in your business.

13. BE HUMBLE: To be humble is to be modest, not proud or arrogant. A truly humble man will not think that he is better than others. He gives honor to everyone. He does not speak arrogantly. He is teachable, and he avoids discord. He is a lover of peace. Promotion lies in the valley of humility. "And whosoever shall exalt himself shall be abased: and he that shall humble himself shall be exalted" (Matthew 23:12). One of the secrets of the greatness of Moses was his humility. He was the most humble man on earth in his days. "Now the man Moses was very meek, above all the men which were upon the face of the earth" (Numbers 12:3). Our Lord Jesus taught us that, for us to be great in the kingdom of God, we must be humble like a child. That means; we must be trusting, we must be lowly in heart, we must be loving and we must be forgiving. "Whosoever, therefore, shall humble himself as this little child, the same is greatest in the kingdom of heaven" (Matthew 18:4). God guides the humble and shows him his ways. "The meek will he guide in judgment: and the meek will he teach his way" (Psalm 25:9). He guides the humble man because the humble man always obeys his instructions. He will not question God, nor refuse his instructions. Abraham is a good example of a humble man, God told him to sacrifice his son Isaac, and Abraham did not argue with God. The Bible recorded that Abraham always obeyed God. Let me ask you this question, do you always obey the Lord's instructions? If you are humble-hearted, God will always guide you and he will teach you his secrets. The wealth of the proud and arrogant shall be given to the humble. "But the meek shall inherit the earth: and shall delight themselves in the abundance of peace" (Psalm 37:11).

14. BE WISE: To be wise is to fear the Lord and to run away from sins. "The fear of the Lord is the beginning of wisdom: a good understanding has all they that do his commandments: his praise endureth forever" (Psalm 111:10). It also means, to have or show experience, knowledge, and good judgment. Wisdom can take a man from nothing to the throne. Wisdom took Joseph from the prison to the throne. "And Pharaoh said unto Joseph, Forasmuch as, God hath shewed thee all this, there is none so discreet and wise as thou art: Thou shall be over my house, and according to unto thy word shall all my people be ruled: only in the throne will I be greater than thou" (Genesis 41:39-40). "A wise servant shall have rule over a son that causeth shame and shall have part of the inheritance among the brethren" (Proverbs 17:2) The wisdom of the wise will make him inherit glory. "The wise shall inherit glory: but shame shall be the promotion of fools" (Proverbs 3:35). If you want to shine, be wise! "And they that be wise shall shine as the brightness of the firmaments..." (Daniel 12:3).

15. YOU NEED A MENTOR: A mentor is a wise and trusted counselor or teacher. The importance of a mentor cannot be overstated. A Mentor inspires you, stretches you, connects you, develops you, and guides and guides you. You need a mentor, especially early in your career. So that he can guide you with his rich experience. Find an experienced mentor in your field of calling, that holds the same values as you and give him the right to mentor you.

Benefits of having a mentor

- Mentors Kick start your professional advancement.
- Mentors help you to clarify and set goals.
- Mentors help you develop your skills.
- Mentors are valuable sources of knowledge.
- Mentors offer constructive criticism.
- Mentors look for ways to promote your personal growth.
- Mentors can help you grow a professional network; they can connect you to others.
- Mentors can inspire you and keep you focused.
- Mentors are disciplinarians that create necessary boundaries that we cannot set for ourselves.
- Mentors are trusted, advisers.

❓ Mentors will guide you until your light begin to shine in your field of calling. "He that walks with wise men shall be wise: but a companion of fools shall be destroyed" (Proverbs 13:20). Apart from mentors, you also need a spiritual Father. A spiritual Father is a spiritual teacher or guide. A spiritual Father will focus on your spiritual enrichment and development. You are to submit to him and honor him. When you have spiritual problems, you are to run to your spiritual Father, not to your mentor. Through the grace of God upon him, he will guide and teach you, until you become spiritually mature. "Unto Timothy, my son in the faith…" (1 Timothy 1:2).

16. FORGIVE OTHERS: To forgive is to cease to feel angry or resentful towards someone or a group of people for an offense, flaw, or mistake. Our Lord Jesus taught us that, if we don't forgive those who offended us, our heavenly Father will not forgive our sins. "But if ye forgive not men their trespasses, neither will your Father forgive your trespasses" (Matthew 6:15). Unforgiveness leads to stagnancy. If you want to move forward in life, forgive and move on. It does not mean that the offender will go unpunished. What God is saying is that, don't revenge, let me do it for you. "To me belongeth vengeance..." (Deuteronomy 32:35). There are some people whom you've sincerely forgiven but you need to keep a distance from. This is because they are like leopards that can not change their spots. "Can the Ethiopian change his skin, or the leopard his spots? then may ye also do good, that is accustomed to doing evil" (Jeremiah 13:23). What you can do to help such people, is to continue to pray for them. So that God can change their hearts for the better. Genuine forgiveness can open doors of blessings and promotion for you. After Job forgave his friends and prayed for them, the Lord promoted Job and blessed him greatly. "And the LORD turned the captivity of Job when he prayed for his friends: also the LORD gave Job twice as much as he had before" (Job 42:10).

17. HAVE FAITH IN GOD: "Now faith is the substance of things hoped for, the evidence of things not seen" (Hebrew 11:1). Faith is also, complete trust or confidence in God. Have faith in God, that he will fulfill all that he has promised to do for you concerning your vision in life. Believe that the glorious future you saw with your eyes of faith shall be fulfilled in due season. The elders of the faith, both old and in the present, obtained their testimonies through their faith in God. If you can have faith in God, what he did for the elders, he will do also for you. He is not a man that will lie, he will do what he says he will do. "For by it the elders obtained a good report" (Hebrew 11:2). "God is not a man, that he should lie; neither the son of man, that he should repent: hath he said, and shall he not do it? or hath he spoken, and shall he not make it good?" (Numbers 23:19). For your faith to produce results, it must not waver and you must add works to your faith. "Let us hold fast the profession of our faith without wavering; for he is faithful that promised" (Hebrews 10:23). "For as the body without the spirit is dead, so faith without works is dead also" (James 2:26). For you to see the glory of God, you must believe that God can help make your dream a reality. "Jesus saith unto her, Said I not unto thee, that if thou wouldest believe, thou shouldest see the glory of God?" (John 11:40). If you have faith in God, you will do great works for his kingdom and your light will shine. "And Jesus said unto them, Because of your unbelief: for verily I say unto you, If ye have faith as a grain of mustard seed, ye shall say unto this mountain, Remove hence to yonder place: and it shall remove, and nothing shall be impossible unto you" (Matthew 17:20).

18. KEEP YOUR EYES FOCUSED ON JESUS:

To keep your eyes focused on Jesus means, To make Jesus the center of your interest. You can do this by looking unto Jesus through the word of God, through prayer and faith. When you keep your gaze on Jesus, you will walk above all difficult situations and you will not sink into problems. If you lose focus, you will be submerged. "And Peter answered him and said, Lord, if it is thou, bid me come unto thee on the water. And he said, come. And when Peter was come down out of the ship, he walked on the water, to go to Jesus. But when he saw the wind boisterous, he was afraid: and beginning to sink, he cried, saying, Lord, save me" (Matthew 14:28-30). When Peter kept his gaze on Jesus, he was walking on the water, but when he shifted focus to the boisterous wind, he began to sink. If you want to shine, keep your gaze on Jesus. "They looked unto him, and were lightened: and their faces were not ashamed" (Psalm 34:5). "But we all, with open face beholding as in a glass the glory of the Lord, are changed into the same image from glory to glory, even as by the spirit of the Lord" (2 Corinthians 3:18). This scripture is saying that we all with faces that have been unveiled, as we look on Jesus, through the word of God, as in a mirror, we shall begin to reflect the glory we see. The spirit of God will keep transforming us from one level of glory to another until we become like him.

19. BE PATIENT: To be patient is to be able to wait on the Lord, without losing your faith and temper, until he fulfills all that he has promised you. A patient person will remain calm while waiting on the Lord. "I waited patiently for the Lord, and he inclined unto me, and heard my cry" (Psalm 40:1). Wait for the Lord, don't go and seek for solution in the wrong places. It will only multiply your sorrow. "Their sorrows shall be multiplied that hasten after another God..." (Psalm 16:4). "The blessing of the Lord, it maketh rich, and he added no sorrow with it" (Proverbs 10:22). The period of waiting, is the period that God uses, to prepare you for the miracle you are expecting. There are lessons that God will teach you, during your waiting period. The earlier you learn your lessons, the better it will be for you. Use your period of waiting to get closer to God. Pray often and study the word of God regularly. When you have now become mature, to manage the blessings and your desired miracles, the Lord will release them to you. "But let patience have her perfect work, that ye may be perfect and entire, wanting nothing" (James 1:4).

8

BENEFITS OF GLORY

1. YOU WILL BE OUTSTANDING: To be outstanding is to be prominent or noticeable; standing out from others. Glory is of different kinds, your glory is different from that of others. It is your manifested glory, that will make you stand out from the crowd. No glory is the same as yours in the whole world. The Glory of Daniel, made him stand out from others in the Land of Babylon. "Then this Daniel was preferred above the presidents and princes, because an excellent spirit was in him, and the king thought to set him over the whole realm" (Daniel 6:3). The glory of Joseph made him outstanding in the land of Egypt. "And Pharaoh said unto Joseph, For as much as God hath shewed thee all this, there is none so discreet and wise as thou art" (Genesis 41:39). To be outstanding also means, to outshine others, you cannot shine without glory. "Arise, shine, for thy light is come, and the glory of the LORD rises upon thee" (Isaiah 60:1).

2. YOU WILL BECOME A RELEVANT PERSON: A relevant person, is the person on whom others depend, whether for leadership, expertise, acumen, or spiritual support. He is a problem solver. The glory of Gideon made him relevant in the land of Israel. "Then the men of Israel said unto Gideon, Rule thou over us, both thou, and thy son, and thy sons also, for thou hast delivered us from the hand of Midian" (Judges 8:22). The glory of Solomon made him relevant on the earth during his days. "And there came of all people to hear the wisdom of Solomon, from all kings of the earth, which had heard of his wisdom" (1 Kings 4:34).

3. YOU WILL BECOME RICH: To be rich is to have lots of money and possessions. A man whose glory is shining will always be blessed with the good things of life. His relevance to society makes people bless him with gifts. In other words, they will always make provision for his needs. "And Johanna the wife of Chuza Herod's stewards, and Susanna, and many others, which ministered unto him of their substance" (Luke 8:3). The glory of Daniel made him a rich man in the land of Babylon. "Then the king made Daniel a great man and gave him many great gifts..." (Daniel 2:48). In Isaiah chapter 60:1, it says: "Arise shine, for thy light, is come, and the glory of the Lord rises upon thee." By the time your glory starts shining, what will follow is an immeasurable blessing towards you. "Then thou see, and flow together and thine heart shall fear, and be enlarge because the abundance of the sea shall be converted unto thee the forces of the Gentiles shall come unto thee" (Isaiah 60:5).

4. YOU WILL BE LIKE JESUS: To be like Jesus is to look exactly like him. To shine like him, to do the works that he did. The disciples of Jesus were first called Christians in Antioch because their lifestyle and speech were like that of Christ. "And the disciples were called Christians first in Antioch" (Acts 11:26). They also shone like Christ, because of the great works that were done through their hands. "And fear came upon every soul: and many wonders and signs were done by the apostles" (Acts 2:43). The more you are transformed from glory to glory. The more you will look like Christ until Christ is fully formed in you. Then you will look like him in glory. "But we all, with open face beholding as in a glass the glory of the Lord are changed into the same image from glory to glory, even as by the spirit of the Lord" (2 Corinthians 3:18). When you are transformed as Jesus, and you are shining like him in glory. Jesus will give you the morning star, and your glory will bring you face to face with the highest GOD!